Mar 2016

D1710000

PIRATES AROUND THE WORLD

Terror on the High Seas

François L'Olonnais

David Derovan

Mitchell Lane
PUBLISHERS
P.O. Box 196
Hockessin, DE 19707
www.mitchelllane.com

PUBLISHERS

Printing   1   2   3   4   5   6   7   8

Anne Bonny
Black Bart (Bartholomew Roberts)
Blackbeard (Edward Teach)
François L'Olonnais

Long Ben (Henry Every)
Sir Francis Drake
Sir Henry Morgan
William Kidd

Library of Congress Cataloging-in-Publication Data
Derovan, David Jay.
 François L'Olonnais / by David Derovan.
    pages cm. — (Pirates around the world : terror on the high seas)
 Includes bibliographical references and index.
 ISBN 978-1-68020-079-9 (library bound)
 1. L'Olonnais, 1630-1671—Juvenile literature. 2. Pirates—Biography—Juvenile literature. I. Title.
 G537.L26D47 2016
 9140.4'5—dc23
 [B]
                                                              2015003193

eBook ISBN: 978-1-68020-080-5

PBP

Contents

Words in **bold** throughout can be found in the Glossary.

Introduction
Left for Dead

Francois L'Olonnais (fran-SWA le-oh-lo-NAY) lay wounded and bleeding, surrounded by the dead bodies of most of his pirate crew. They had been shipwrecked, though and he and most of his crew had been washed ashore and survived. However, Spanish soldiers soon discovered them and the next thing they knew, the pirates were fighting for their lives.

They were overwhelmed and most of the pirates were killed. Out of the corner of his eye, L'Olonnais saw the Spanish soldiers gathering the survivors further down the beach, close to the entrance to the forest. Seeing that their backs were turned to him, he gathered sand and rubbed it into the blood oozing from his wounds. Moving very slowly, he reached out and pulled one of the dead men closer so that he was partly covered by the body. He closed his eyes and slowed his breathing.

Campeche, Mexico

A few minutes later, he heard the Spanish soldiers walking among the dead pirates. He understood enough Spanish to know that they were looking for him. Finally one of the Spaniards said, "Look! There he is! François L'Olonnais is dead."

Having confirmed his death, the Spanish soldiers turned and marched their prisoners toward the town of Campeche, a prosperous town on the western coast of the Yucatan Peninsula in modern-day Mexico.

Escaping Campeche at Night

L'Olonnais remained where he was for several more hours, until the forest began to cast long shadows over the bloody beach. Carefully he opened his eyes and squinted to see if the Spaniards had left a guard behind. They hadn't. All the Spaniards were gone. Slowly, he sat up and then rose to his feet. Some of his wounds were still dripping blood. L'Olonnais walked into the forest. Before long, he found a stream where he washed his wounds and cleaned himself. He wrapped his wounds with long leaves and sat down to rest with his cutlass next to him.[1]

The night passed. L'Olonnais did not sleep well. His wounds bothered him. As the sun rose the next morning, he felt better but he was still very weak. He was alone, deep in enemy territory.

Two mornings later, L'Olonnais was strong enough to walk to Campeche. On the edge of town, he passed a shack with men's clothes hanging out to dry. L'Olonnais helped himself to a pair of pants and a rough shirt. Along with the straw hat he stole, he now looked like all the other Spanish peasants, the poor people who farmed the land.

L'Olonnais discovered that the townspeople of Campeche were celebrating the death of the horrible pirate, François L'Olonnais! Well, he certainly knew better!

Late in the afternoon, L'Olonnais talked with some slaves near the harbor. He offered them freedom if they would steal a canoe from their master so they could escape together from Campeche. Since he promised them freedom, they agreed to help him.

That night, L'Olonnais and his new friends loaded up the canoe with fresh water and food. Quietly, slowly, carefully they paddled out of the harbor. François L'Olonnais was free again to live the life of a pirate.[2]

This is one of the few images of François L'Olonnais. It was created in 1678.

François L'Olonnais Who?

Francois L'Olonnais was born in France around 1635. His parents named him Jean David Nau. When he was growing up, the world was changing constantly. The three main countries in Europe—Spain, England and France—were fighting wars with each other all the time. These conflicts spilled over into the newly discovered Americas.

Around the age of 15 he came to the Caribbean as an **indentured servant**.[1] An indentured servant was a person who signed a contract to work for a master in America. The length of the contract was usually five to seven years. Very poor people, like Jean David Nau, became indentured servants in the hope of eventually making a new life for themselves.[2]

Jean David Nau finished his seven years and had to decide what to do next. Returning to France was out of the question. Life was so tough in England and France in those days that many young men became sailors because there were no other jobs.[3] So, after his contract was up, Nau joined a band of **buccaneers** in Tortuga, an island off the northwest coast of Hispaniola (which is shared by the modern-day countries of the Dominican Republic and Haiti),[4] and changed his name to François L'Olonnais.[5] His new last name reflected Olonne, the name of the region in France where he had been born.

CHAPTER 1

Becoming a Cruel Privateer

Very quickly, L'Olonnais's reputation for courage grew to the extent that the governor of Tortuga, Monsieur de la Place, actually gave him a ship and a license to capture Spanish ships and steal their treasure.

At first, he was very successful. He seized many Spanish ships and became rich.[6]

L'Olonnais hated the Spanish and he was very cruel to the sailors of the ships he captured. He and his men would kill almost the entire crew, only leaving one or two men alive to spread the word throughout the Caribbean that François L'Olonnais was someone to fear. When Spanish sailors realized that L'Olonnais was about to attack their ship, many of them jumped overboard because they did not want to be tortured by him,[7] even though most sailors in those days did not know how to swim.

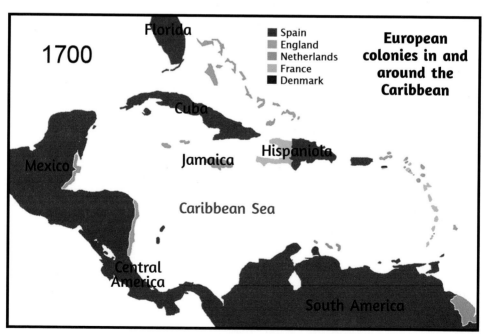

The Caribbean Sea surrounded by the Spanish Main (in red).

The Caribbean Sea and the Spanish Main

In 1492, Christopher Columbus explored some of the islands of the Caribbean Sea, which separates North America from South America. He claimed all of the islands and lands he discovered for Spain. The Pope agreed and declared Spain as the ruler of these new lands.[8]

By 1502, just ten years after Columbus's first voyage, Spain already had settlements and towns on several of the islands in the Caribbean Sea.[9] They continued to explore the area, finding what is today Mexico and other parts of Central and South America. The English called the lands surrounding the Caribbean Sea the Spanish Mainland, which was shortened to the Spanish Main.[10]

England, France, Portugal, and the Dutch were not happy that Spain claimed all of the newly discovered lands. They also became aware that the Spanish were beginning to ship large amounts of gold and silver from these new lands back to Spain. They desired a share in all of this wealth.

The easiest way of obtaining a share of this wealth was to steal it. In 1521, the first act of piracy was led by Jean Fleury, a Frenchman who attacked three large Spanish ships filled with gold, silver and jewels. Fleury took his loot back to France and became a hero. Jean Fleury was the first pirate of the Caribbean![11]

Christopher Columbus

A seventeenth-century illustration of the harbor of Havana, Cuba.

"I Shall Never Give Quarter to Any Spaniard"

Francois L'Olonnais was a great success as a pirate. However, he soon ran into trouble. There was a huge storm and his ship sank not far from Campeche, which resulted in his being wounded and eventual escape.

He returned to Tortuga, where he became captain of another ship. L'Olonnais and his new crew headed for de los Cayos, a prosperous trading village along the southern coast of Cuba. Apparently, people in those days were always on the lookout for pirates. The villagers recognized L'Olonnais in time to run away. While in hiding, the villagers sent a letter to the governor in the colony's capital in Havana asking for help because their village was under attack by L'Olonnais.

The governor didn't believe them at first because he just received a letter from Campeche saying L'Olonnais was dead! Nevertheless, he sent a ship with fifty soldiers to capture L'Olonnais. The force also included an African slave whose job was to hang the pirates.

Attacking the Spanish Ship with Canoes!
François L'Olonnais saw them coming. Since the harbor at de los Cayos was too shallow for their ship, the Spaniards anchored outside the harbor. That evening L'Olonnais and several men rowed over in a canoe to meet the ship. When

the soldiers on the ship asked who they were and if they
had seen the famous pirate, François L'Olonnais, one of the
men with L'Olonnais answered that the pirates had fled.
The soldiers relaxed.

Just before dawn, L'Olonnais attacked the ship with two
canoes filled with pirates. They caught the Spanish sentries
off guard. The sounds of the battle woke up the rest of the
soldiers and the crew. It was a bloody battle, but the pirates

This 1670 painting shows enslaved Africans working in the tobacco sheds on a colonial tobacco plantation.

managed to drive the Spaniards below the main deck of the ship. One by one, L'Olonnais had them come up. One by one he killed them. Then the African slave came up to the main deck. He pleaded with L'Olonnais to spare his life. In return, he offered to tell L'Olonnais everything. François agreed and the African slave told him that the governor of Cuba had sent them to hunt down and kill all the pirates. He also told L'Olonnais that he had been given the job of

There are no images of the actual ship that François L'Olonnais commanded. It may have been similar to these vessels.

hanging the pirates. After hearing what the slave had to say, L'Olonnais ordered him to be killed.

L'Olonnais allowed only one Spaniard to live. He sent the man back to the governor of Cuba with this message: "I shall never henceforth (from now on) give quarter to any Spaniard whatsoever; and I have great hopes I shall execute on your own person the very same punishment I have done upon them you sent against me."

Needless to say, the governor of Cuba was very unhappy with that message. He vowed to hunt him down, along with all the other pirates who were with him. L'Olonnais never had a chance to make good his threat to kill the governor of Cuba.

Instead, he sailed off. Soon afterwards, he seized another ship filled with a valuable cargo. He then returned to Tortuga to plan his next adventure.[1]

"Give No Quarter" and the Jolly Roger

The phrase, "to give no quarter," means that the pirates would not ask for mercy when fighting and they would show no mercy when they attacked. The earliest pirate flag was a simple red **pennant**—a long, narrow, pointed flag. When ship captains and crews saw another ship approaching flying the red pennant, they knew that they were being chased by pirates who would "give no quarter." As a result, they often gave up without fighting the pirates.[2]

The pirates preferred to seize a ship without fighting. There was no guarantee that the pirates would win every battle. Even if they won, some of their men were likely to die or be seriously wounded. There was always the danger that their ship would be damaged. Therefore, it was much better to scare their enemies into surrendering by flying the red pennant.

Some historians think that the red pennant was called the "jolie rouge" in French, meaning the "pretty red." In English the French words became "Jolly Roger," which became the name given to the black pirate flags that featured skulls and crossed bones or other symbols of death.

Pirates attacking a Spanish galleon.

The Maracaibo Raid

Francois L'Olonnais had a great idea that he sold to the pirates of Tortuga. This idea was to raid the town of Maracaibo (in modern-day Venezuela). Maracaibo was known as a very rich town, and every pirate dreamed of its enormous wealth. So many pirates wanted to join him that he managed to put together a **fleet** of eight ships and a small army of six hundred and thirty pirates! He even convinced the governor of Tortuga, a retired pirate named Michael de Basco, to be in charge of the pirate army when they fought on land.

The fleet sailed from Tortuga at the end of July 1667. As they sailed around Hispaniola and headed south, they saw a Spanish galleon approaching. L'Olonnais left the fleet anchored off the southeastern tip of Hispaniola and went off to capture the Spanish ship.

The pirates fought with the Spaniards for three hours. First, they exchanged **broadsides** of cannon fire, interrupted by maneuvering their ships into position to fire more broadsides. Finally, the pirates boarded the Spanish ship and fought hand-to-hand with swords and **pistols** until the Spaniards surrendered. L'Olonnais sent the captured ship back to Tortuga with orders that it return to him after all the **merchandise** was unloaded.

While waiting for L'Olonnais, the rest of the pirates spotted another Spanish ship. They captured it and discovered that it was loaded with fresh water and food. Just the kind of supplies they needed. The fleet regrouped and encouraged by their successes, they headed for Maracaibo.[1]

Attacking Maracaibo

To get there, they entered the **Gulf** of Venezuela, along the northern coast of modern-day Venezuela. At the southern end of the gulf are a number of very small islands that separate the gulf from another body of water to the south: Lake Maracaibo, a freshwater lake that is the biggest lake in South America.[2] The town of Maracaibo lay just south of those small islands, at the entrance to the lake. One of the islands had a tall watchtower. At the top of another island was a fort guarding the only channel that led to the town. It consisted of large mounds of dirt and sixteen large cannons.

L'Olonnais and his fleet sailed south through the Gulf of Venezuela until they were close to Maracaibo. Then they dropped anchor and spent the night out of sight of the watchtower and the fort. Early the following morning they went ashore. Despite the efforts of the pirates at secrecy, their arrival had been discovered. So the Spaniards set up an ambuscade—an ambush manned by soldiers behind barricades—along the only path leading to the fort.

L'Olonnais and his men ran right over the ambuscade. The Spaniards fled for their lives and headed to Maracaibo, while L'Olonnais and his pirate army marched up the hill and attacked the fort. Using their swords and pistols, the pirates once again fought for hours until they managed to conquer the fort. Now there was nothing to stop them from attacking Maracaibo.

While L'Olonnais and his crew were busy destroying the fort, the surviving Spanish soldiers arrived in the town of Maracaibo and raised the alarm, telling the terrified inhabitants that L'Olonnais was on his way with two thousand men—several times the actual size of his force. So they gathered everything they had that was valuable. Some fled into the forest that surrounded the town, while others sailed in whatever small boats they could find down the lake to the town of Gibraltar.

Map of Lake Maracaibo showing the towns along its shore

CHAPTER 3

Looting Maracaibo

The next morning, L'Olonnais set sail with the fleet for Maracaibo, but there was hardly any wind. It took another whole day until they arrived in Maracaibo. Imagine how surprised the pirates must have been to find the town deserted! The men gorged themselves on the vast amounts of delicious food that the townspeople had left behind in their hurry to escape.

L'Olonnais was one smart pirate. He sent a group of one hundred and sixty men into the forest to find the townspeople who had fled. That night, his men returned with some gold coins and jewels, mules loaded with merchandise, and twenty prisoners. L'Olonnais threatened the prisoners with the most horrible torture so they would reveal where the other townspeople were hiding. He proved that he wasn't bluffing when he hacked one of the unfortunate prisoners to death with his sword. His cruelty didn't work out, because the rest of the people hiding in the forest moved to other locations after burying their money and valuables in places where the pirates would never find them.

So far, L'Olonnais's little venture at mass robbery had not been very successful. After fifteen days of resting and feasting in Maracaibo, the pirates set sail for Gibraltar, near the other end of the lake. They hoped they might find more treasure there.

pirate sword

The Spanish Galleon

Starting in the 1500s, Spanish businessmen shipped their merchandise on a special kind of ship called the Spanish galleon. The first Spanish galleons were relatively small ships, but by the 1700s they had become much larger. Like all ships in those days, the galleons were built out of wood and were propelled by the winds.

Viewed from the back, the galleon had a somewhat roundish shape. Viewed from the side, the galleon was low in front (the **bow**) and built up in the back (the **stern**). The galleon had two or three **masts** with square-rigged sails, as well as one triangular (lateen) sail on the short mast at the stern.

Since the galleons were often used to transport large amounts of gold and silver and other precious cargoes from the Spanish Main across the Atlantic Ocean to Spain, they were armed with cannons and had soldiers on board to protect the ship and its contents. Attacking such large and well-armed ships was always a challenge. However, the pirates knew that if they captured the ship, then the result would make them all rich.[3]

The design of the galleons was so successful that British, French, and Dutch shipbuilders copied the design.

A wooden model of a Spanish galleon from the Museo Storico Navale di Venezia (Naval History Museum) in Venice, Italy

The damage inflicted upon Gibraltar by L'Olonnais and his men was so great that the city, formerly a major center for the exportation of cacao, nearly ceased to exist by 1680.

On to Gibraltar

While L'Olonnais and his men were enjoying Maracaibo, the people of Gibraltar—along with the refugees from Maracaibo—appealed to the governor of neighboring Mérida for help. He immediately sent four hundred soldiers. In addition, hundreds of townspeople armed themselves and joined the soldiers. Under the governor's guidance, they built a dirt fort where they placed cannons pointing out to sea. Then they constructed a barricade along the only road leading into Gibraltar.

Even though L'Olonnais knew he couldn't sneak up on Gibraltar, he was determined to capture the city and the riches he believed it contained despite being badly outnumbered. He even threatened to kill any of his men who hesitated to attack.

Right away he ran into a problem. He didn't know the best way of approaching the town and led his men into a bog, where some Spanish horsemen discovered them and began shooting. The pirates were resourceful and quickly cut down branches to make a crude roadway that enabled them to reach solid ground.

Let the Fighting Begin!

Now they faced another serious obstacle. Once the pirates emerged from the woods on the road leading to the town,

they found the barricade that the Spaniards had erected. The Spaniards opened fire with **muskets**, pistols, and cannons filled with bullets and small jagged pieces of metal. As a result, a number of pirates were wounded or killed.

L'Olonnais and his men searched for another way into town but could not find one. When they returned to the main road, the Spaniards resumed their firing. The pirates could not get around them.

That is when L'Olonnais used a very old trick. He and his men turned and ran away from the Spaniards. Many of the Spaniards came out from behind their barricade and chased the pirates down the road. Before they realized what they had done, the pirates turned on them and attacked them, killing at least two hundred of their enemies. The rest ran into the woods. L'Olonnais returned to the barricade where the remaining Spaniards surrendered.

L'Olonnais had captured Gibraltar. The pirates gathered the townspeople in the church. They discovered that over five hundred Spaniards had died in the fighting, along with others who died of their wounds in the woods. Only forty pirates died in the battle and another eighty were wounded. In time, many of those wounded also died. All of the dead pirates were piled into two small boats that were dragged out into the middle of the lake and sunk.

Back to Maracaibo for More Gold

At the same time, other pirates turned the area around the church into a fort, in case the Spaniards came back to attack them. When that didn't happen, L'Olonnais and his men started looking for money and valuables. Unfortunately for the pirates, there wasn't very much left to steal. Again, L'Olonnais proved to be smart. He sent four prisoners into the woods to deliver a ransom demand message to all those

A colored engraving of a musketeer by Dutch artist Jacques de Gheyn in 1607. Notice the pole in his left hand that is used to support the front of the musket when it is fired.

hiding there, threatening to burn the town if they didn't meet his demand. The Spaniards had two days to pay the ransom, but they couldn't collect the whole amount in time. So, L'Olonnais started to burn certain sections of the town, though he allowed his Spanish prisoners to put out most of the fires. As a result, he immediately received the ransom money. The pirates packed up the money and valuables and left Gibraltar. They headed back to Maracaibo.

When L'Olonnais and his fleet of pirate ships anchored in the Maracaibo harbor, the townspeople who had returned to their homes became hysterical. L'Olonnais sent them a message that he wanted 30,000 gold pieces as a ransom. Pay it and he would go away. The Spaniards negotiated the ransom down to 20,000 gold pieces, which they paid along with giving five hundred cows to the pirates. The pirates sailed away and the people of Maracaibo breathed easier. Three days later, L'Olonnais and his ships were back! Once again the town was in an uproar. L'Olonnais sent a message that all he wanted was a **pilot** who would guide his ships safely out of the lake and into the gulf. The townspeople immediately sent L'Olonnais a pilot.

Splitting the Loot

Eight days later, the pirate fleet docked at a small island off Hispaniola called Cow Island. They unloaded all of the money and

A pirate captain talks with several captives.

valuables they had stolen during the two months they had spent in Lake Maracaibo. Aside from all kinds of valuable cloth and other merchandise, they had taken 260,000 gold coins. After a very careful accounting, each pirate received his share of the loot. Then they returned to Tortuga to tell their tales and to spend their money. There were plenty of ways to spend it. They ate huge amounts of food and flocked to the taverns, where they loved to drink. Many of them gambled away the wealth they had amassed from the raids. Within three weeks nearly all of the pirates had lost their money. L'Olonnais had to come up with a way for these men to enrich themselves again.[1]

Gold Spanish coins similar to the ones L'Olonnais divided with his pirate crew.

Pistols and Muskets

Besides their swords, the most important weapons pirates carried were pistols and muskets. To load them, pirates would pour a small amount of explosive powder into the barrel. Then a round metal ball (sometimes two or even three) would be put into the barrel in front of the powder. The ball and powder were held in place with wadding, a small piece of cloth shoved down the barrel by a thin, straight metal rod called a **ramrod**.

A pistol could only shoot one bullet at a time. For this reason many pirates wore a baldric, a wide piece of leather across the chest with leather strips for holstering their pistols. After shooting a pistol, it was returned to the baldric so it could be reloaded during a lull in the action.

When boarding another ship, the pirates sometimes used a musket with a very short barrel called a musketoon, Another kind of musket used by pirates was a blunderbuss. It had a wider barrel and could be loaded with pellets, scraps of metal, and glass. It was a nasty weapon, especially in hand-to-hand battles.

The biggest problem with pistols and muskets was keeping the powder dry while at sea. If it got wet or damp, the weapons would not fire. Needless to say, many pirates practiced firing these weapons until they could shoot very accurately.[2]

West European flint gun of the 17th century.

A beautiful 1855 first edition example of J.H. Colton's map of Central America.

Disaster in Central America

With his great success in the Maracaibo raid, François L'Olonnais had no trouble gathering recruits and ships for his next venture—an attack on Nicaragua. He assembled a fleet of six ships and a force of seven hundred men.

At first, everything went well. They stopped at Bahaya, on Hispaniola, to load up supplies and then at a Cuban fishing village to steal canoes. L'Olonnais knew that they would need canoes where they were going because their ships could not travel up the rivers along the coast.

Then things started to fall apart. Without wind, sailing ships cannot move. After leaving Cuba, L'Olonnais and his friends literally ran out of wind. They were also running out of fresh water and food. The currents pushed the fleet into the Gulf of Honduras, where they anchored in the first place they could. Using their canoes, they entered the Xagua River and attacked the Indian villages.

The Indians were no match for the pirates, who killed the Indians throughout the region and destroyed their villages. However, the invaders did not find much to eat—just some grain, hogs, and chickens. They went back to the coastline and headed west. Soon they came to a Spanish settlement called Puerto Cavallo. A good-sized ship armed with twenty-four cannons and sixteen pateraras (small

cannons) was anchored there. The pirates easily captured the vessel.

Then they burned two warehouses filled with merchandise that was to be shipped to Spain.

Cruelty and Torture

L'Olonnais and his pirate army were very cruel people. They killed almost everyone they could find. The ones they captured were tortured so they would tell the pirates where all the gold and valuables were hidden. Only two people revealed where they had hidden their money.

So far, the pirates had very little to show for their efforts. L'Olonnais decided to take three hundred men and march inland to a town called San Pedro. He left the rest of his men in Puerto Cavallo.

Just three miles down the road, L'Olonnais and his men came to an ambuscade, a strong barricade manned by Spanish soldiers. L'Olonnais and the pirates defeated this group of soldiers, but some of their men were killed and wounded. Many Spanish soldiers died as well. L'Olonnais killed all the wounded Spaniards, but some ran away to warn the town of San Pedro that the pirates were coming.

Before continuing to march toward San Pedro, L'Olonnais asked the surviving Spaniards if there were more ambuscades along the road. They said, "Yes." Then he asked them one by one if there was another path into San Pedro. At first they said, "No," but after L'Olonnais began to torture them they finally agreed to show him another path.

It wasn't long before L'Olonnais realized that this alternative path was not passable. He and his men were forced to return to the main road. L'Olonnais was furious.

After looting a town, the pirates are unhappy that they come away with so little of value.

He grabbed one of the prisoners and murdered him in a particularly gruesome way.

Fighting Their Way to San Pedro

Even on a good day, L'Olonnais was a nasty man. Now that his plans were falling apart, he became even more cruel. The pirates proceeded down the road and found the next ambuscade. They were so angry and frustrated that in a half an hour they defeated the Spanish soldiers. Many Spaniards died and the rest ran back to San Pedro.

Even pirates have to rest, so L'Olonnais and his men waited until the next day to continue toward San Pedro. Soon, they found a third ambuscade in their way. This time, the pirates threw fireballs at the Spanish soldiers and then attacked them. An hour later it was all over. L'Olonnais thought that the road was clear for him to enter San Pedro.

However, when they arrived at the outskirts of the town, they found that the Spaniards had set up yet another barricade. Both sides fought with muskets and pistols. The pirates let the Spanish soldiers and townspeople fire first. Then L'Olonnais's men threw fireballs at the Spaniards. This was followed by hand-to-hand combat with swords and axes. The Spaniards still did not give up. The pirates had to **retreat**. Again the pirates attacked, with fewer men. These pirates made every shot count, resulting in many dead Spaniards.

Through all of the confusion, the smoke, the cries of the wounded, the pirates attacked again and again. The fighting lasted all day. Finally, at night, the Spaniards put up a white flag and asked to **parley** with the pirates.

The Spaniards offered to give up their town, but in return they asked for two hours in order to gather their valuables and run away into the forest. L'Olonnais agreed. When the time was up, L'Olonnais sent his men into the forest to capture the townspeople and steal their valuables. The pirates were not very successful in finding the Spaniards or their valuables. Frustrated and disappointed, L'Olonnais and his men spent the next five days in San Pedro stealing whatever they could and then burning the town to the ground. Now, it was back to Puerto Cavallo and the sea.

Back to Sea

Arriving at the coast, L'Olonnais discovered that the men he left there had been busy attacking fishing villages. Then they heard that a large Spanish ship was expected in Puerto Cavallo. L'Olonnais joined them and decided on what to do next. He left a couple of canoes filled with his men to warn him of the coming of the merchant ship. Meanwhile, he sailed with his ships up the coast of the Yucatan Peninsula. He came to the Isle of Sambale where he **careened** his ship and had his men make ropes out of a native plant called macoa.

After two months of fixing his ships and making ropes, L'Olonnais got word that the Spanish merchant ship had finally arrived. Hurrying down the coast, L'Olonnais arrived in the harbor with his fleet to find the Spanish ship unloading its cargo. The Spanish ship had over forty cannons, as well as two hundred and fifty soldiers on board with muskets. L'Olonnais attacked anyway, but was beaten back by the well-equipped Spaniards. Not willing to give up, L'Olonnais sent four canoes filled with pirates to attack the big ship while the harbor air was filled with the smoke from all the cannon fire. The pirates quietly climbed aboard and quickly took over the ship.

Nevertheless, this was another moment of frustration and disappointment for L'Olonnais. The big ship carried very little of real value for the pirates.

L'Olonnais called for a council meeting of all the men from his entire fleet. So far, they had not accomplished very much and had not accumulated much gold or valuables. L'Olonnais announced that he wanted to raid the towns in Guatemala. The majority of the men decided to leave L'Olonnais and to go elsewhere. These pirates sailed to what is today Costa Rica. They attacked the town of Veraguas and came away with very little. So they marched overland south to the town of Nata, which is on the Pacific Ocean coast of Costa Rica. Realizing that the Spaniards were waiting for them with a large group of soldiers, they retreated and sailed back to Tortuga.[1]

Photo of a vintage cannon aboard a ship. The ropes keep the cannon from flying across the deck after it has been fired.

Careening a Ship

Hundreds of years ago, the bottoms of wooden ships had to be repaired and cleaned. Most of the time, ship crews did this far away from any **drydock**, a place where the water could be temporarily removed so the crews could work on the bottom of the ship.

Therefore, when it was time to perform this necessary chore, the crew would sail the ship close to the shore and wait for **high tide**. When the tide ran out, sailors pulled the ship to one side, allowing them work on one side of the ship's bottom. This is called careening a ship. When they finished one side, they floated the ship again as the tide came in. Then they waited for **low tide** and pulled the ship to the other side.[2]

Three things required the sailors' attention. First, they had to remove any weeds or **barnacles** that had attached themselves to the bottom of the ship. These weeds and barnacles slowed down the ship as it moved through the water. Second, they had to patch any holes in the wood in the bottom of the ship. Third, it was necessary to remove the **teredo** worms that had bored holes in the bottom of the ship.[3]

Once the repairs were made, it was back out to sea!

A piece from a wooden hull eaten away by teredo worms.

Two pirates escape from a battle in a longboat equipped with a mast and sail.

The Final Disaster

L 'Olonnais and his remaining men sailed south along the eastern shore of Nicaragua. Disaster struck when the pirates approached one of the islands in the de las Pertas group. Their ship got stuck on a **sandbar**. Nothing they did allowed the ship to float freely again. They unloaded everything, including the cannons. Nothing worked. The vessel wouldn't budge. The only option left was to break it apart and use the wood to build a new, much smaller vessel.

The pirates spent almost ten months building a sturdy longboat, complete with a mast and sails. L'Olonnais took as many men with him in the longboat as he could and sailed south to the Nicaragua River. Attempting to land there to find some canoes to take back to the men he left behind, L'Olonnais was met by a large group of Spanish soldiers and Indians who worked together to drive the pirates back to sea. More than half of his men were killed. Instead of going back for the men he left behind, L'Olonnais sailed on in search of canoes.

Meanwhile, the men that he left behind were picked up by another pirate ship. This combined group also met disaster. They anchored their ship and headed up one of the rivers to seek valuables and food. All they found was misery. After two weeks without food or water, the survivors struggled back to their ship.

CHAPTER 6

A Nasty End

At the same time, still searching for canoes, L'Olonnais travelled to the Gulf of Darien, which lies between modern-day Panama and Colombia. He was unaware that the Darien Indians were among the most savage Indians on the Spanish Main. Not long after they left their longboat and entered the forest, L'Olonnais and his men were **ferociously** attacked by these Indians. Only one sailor survived by running from the battle. He witnessed the Indians kill L'Olonnais and all the other men. This witness saw the Indians chop up their bodies and then burn them in a giant bonfire.[1]

François L'Olonnais died in the year 1668.[2] He was just 33 years old. His career as a pirate captain lasted for less than ten years.

Today, François L'Olonnais is not as well-known as such pirates as Blackbeard and Captain William Kidd. On the one hand, L'Olonnais was an excellent sailor and navigator. He had the knack of gathering men around him and leading them. On the other hand, he was also a mass murderer who tortured people. He hated Spain and the Spanish people. His only goal in life was to rob and steal as much wealth as he could. He was a nasty pirate who met a particularly cruel death.

The wild jungle near Darien, Colombia, where L'Olonnais met his death.

Alexander Exquemelin

Almost all works about L'Olonnais quote the same source, a book by Alexander Exquemelin (EX-ke-meh-len) titled *The Buccaneers of North America*. Its original title was *The American Sea-Rovers*. Like L'Olonnais, Exquemelin arrived in the Caribbean as an indentured servant. After falling deathly ill, he was sold to a second master, a doctor, who taught Exquemelin to be a doctor. After his term as an indentured servant was completed, his master gave Exquemelin a set of surgical tools, thus launching his career as a doctor.

Exquemelin served as the doctor on various pirate ships, most notably with the famous pirate Henry Morgan. In the late 1670s Exquemelin retired from the pirate life and settled in Amsterdam, Holland. Eventually he passed a series of tests and became an official doctor and surgeon.

In 1678, he published *The Buccaneers of North America*. The book contains a number of chapters about François L'Olonnais.[3] His book was translated into Spanish in 1681 and into English in 1684. The book is considered one of the most important eyewitness accounts of the pirates of the 1600s. Even though Henry Morgan sued Exquemelin for writing lies about him and won his court case, *The Buccaneers of North America* is considered to be true stories of real pirates. It is still published today.[4]

The title page of Exquemelin's book shows its original title, De Americaensche Zee-Roovers *(The American Sea-Rovers).*

Chapter Notes

Introduction: Left for Dead

1. Alexander O. Exquemelin, *The Buccaneers of America* (New York: Digireads.com Book, 2010), pp. 51–53.
2. Ibid.

Chapter 1: François L'Olonnais Who?

1. Cindy Vallar, *Pirates and Privateers: The History of Maritime Piracy.* http://www.cindyvallar.com/lolonnais.html
2. *Dictionary.com,* http://dictionary.reference.com/browse/indentured%20servant?s=t; U.S. History, http://www.ushistory.org/us/5b.asp
3. Alexander O. Exquemelin, *The Buccaneers of America* (New York: Digireads.com Book, 2010), p. 51.
4. Vallar, *Pirates and Privateers.*
5. Gail Selinger and W. Thomas Smith Jr., *The Complete Idiot's Guide to Pirates* (New York: Alpha Books, 2006), p. 104.
6. Ibid., p. 105.
7. Ibid.
8. Ibid., p. 35.
9. Ibid., p. 39.
10. Ibid., p. 40.
11. Ibid., pp. 41–42.

Chapter 2: "I Shall Never Give Quarter to Any Spaniard"

1. Alexander O. Exquemelin, *The Buccaneers of America* (New York: Digireads.com Book, 2010), pp. 53–55.
2. John Matthews, *Pirates* (New York: Atheneum Books, 2006), p. 14.
3. Gail Selinger and W. Thomas Smith Jr., *The Complete Idiot's Guide to Pirates* (New York: Alpha Books, 2006) , p. 196.

Chapter 3: The Maracaibo Raid

1. Alexander O. Exquemelin, *The Buccaneers of America* (New York: Digireads.com Book, 2010), pp. 54–55.
2. *Worldatlas: Explore Your World.* http://www.worldatlas.com/aatlas/infopage/lakemaracaibo.htm
3. Angus Konstam, *The World Atlas of Pirates: Treasures and Treachery on the Seven Seas—in Maps, Tall Tales, and Pictures* (Guilford, CT: The Lyons Press, 2009), p. 65; Vallar, *Pirates and Privateers.*

Chapter Notes

Chapter 4: On to Gibraltar

1. Alexander O. Exquemelin, *The Buccaneers of America* (New York: Digireads.com Book, 2010), pp. 56–62.

2. Gail Selinger and W. Thomas Smith Jr., *The Complete Idiot's Guide to Pirates* (New York: Alpha Books 2006), pp. 179–182; Tobias Gibson, *Pirates of the Caribbean, in Fact and Fiction.* http://pirates.hegewisch.net/pirates.html; Chris Poore, *A Life Before the Mast: A Guide to Recreating Sailors, Privateers & Pirates 1650–1680*, pp. 7–8. http://www.17thcenturylifeandtimes.com/Images/alifebeforethemast.pdf

Chapter 5: Disaster in Central America

1. Alexander O. Exquemelin, *The Buccaneers of America* (New York: Digireads.com Book, 2010), pp. 62–69.

2. Gail Selinger & W. Thomas Smith Jr., *The Complete Idiot's Guide to Pirates* (New York: Alpha Books, 2006), p. 158.

3. Angus Konstam and Tony Bryan, *The Pirate Ship 1660–1730* (Oxford, United Kingdom: Osprey Publishing, 2003), pp. 5–6.

Chapter 6: The Final Disaster

1. Alexander O. Exquemelin, *The Buccaneers of America* (New York: Digireads.com Book, 2010), pp. 69–72; Angus Konstam, *The World Atlas of Pirates: Treasures and Treachery on the Seven Seas — in Maps, Tall Tales, and Pictures* (Guilford, CT: The Lyons Press 2009), pp. 92–93.

2. Gail Selinger and W. Thomas Smith Jr., *The Complete Idiot's Guide to Pirates* (New York: Alpha Books, 2006), p. 106.

3. Angus Konstam, *Piracy: The Complete History* (Oxford, United Kingdom: Osprey Publishing, 2008), p. 109.

4. Selinger and Smith, *The Complete Idiot's Guide to Pirates*, pp. 89–90.

Works Consulted

Botting, Douglas. *The Pirates*. The Seafarers Series. Alexandria, VA: Time-Life Books, 1978.

Exquemelin, Alexander O. *The Buccaneers of America*. New York: Digireads.com Book, New York, 2010.

Gentlemen of Fortune. http://www.gentlemenoffortune.com/.

Gibson, Tobias. *Pirates of the Caribbean, in Fact and Fiction*. http://pirates.hegewisch.net/pirates.html.

Gosse, Philip, *The History of Piracy*. Mineola, NY: Dover Publications, 2007 (reproduction of 1932 edition).

Karg, Barb and Arjean Spaite. T*he Everything Pirates Book: A Swashbuckling History of Adventure on the High Seas*. Avon, MA: Adams Media, 2007.

Konstam, Angus, and Tony Bryan. *The Pirate Ship 1660–1730*. Oxford, United Kingdom: Osprey Publishing, 2003.

Konstam, Angus. *Piracy: The Complete History*. Oxford, United Kingdom: Osprey Publishing, 2008.

Konstam, Angus. *The World Atlas of Pirates: Treasures and Treachery on the Seven Seas—in Maps, Tall Tales, and Pictures*. Guilford, CT: The Lyons Press, 2009.

Langley, Andrew. *100 Things You Should Know about Pirates*. New York: Barnes & Noble, 2000.

"L'Olonnais, François." *Pirates through the Ages Reference Library*. Ed. Jennifer Stock. Vol. 3: Biographies. Detroit: U*X*L, 2011.

Pirateology: The Sea Journal of Captain William Lubber. Dorking, United Kingdom: Templar Publishing, 2006.

Pirates of the Caribbean. http://pirates.hegewisch.net/pirates.html

Poore, Chris. *A Life Before the Mast: A Guide to Recreating Sailors, Privateers & Pirates 1650–1680*. Edited by Ross Davies and Laura Dean. http://www.17thcenturylifeandtimes.com/Images/alifebeforethemast.pdf

Royal Museums Greenwich. http://www.rmg.co.uk/search/gss/Pirates.

Selinger, Gail, and W. Thomas Smith Jr. *The Complete Idiot's Guide to Pirates*. New York: Alpha Books, 2006.

Works Consulted

Stockton, Jack. *Pirates of Our Coast: A History of Pirates and Buccaneers*. Wilmington, NC: Dram Tree Books, 2007.

The Way of the Pirates. http://www.thewayofthepirates.com/famous-pirates/francois-lolonnais.php.

Vallar, Cindy. *Pirates and Privateers: The History of Maritime Piracy*. http://www.cindyvallar.com/pirates.html

Further Reading

Beahm, George. *Caribbean Pirates: A Treasure Chest of Fact, Fiction, and Folklore*. Newburyport, MA: Hampton Roads Publishing, 2007.

Bradman, Tony. *The Kingfisher Treasury of Pirate Stories*. New York: Macmillan Kingfisher Books, 2003.

DragoArt.com. "How to Draw a Pirate Ship. http://www.dragoart.com/tuts/1308/1/1/how-to-draw-a-pirate-ship.htm

Krull, Kathleen, *Lives of the Pirates: Swashbucklers, Scoundrels (Neighbors Beware!)*. Boston: Houghton Mifflin Harcourt Books for Young Readers, 2013.

Langley, Andrew. *100 Things You Should Know about Pirates*. New York: Barnes & Noble, 2000.

Matthews, John. *Pirates*. New York: Atheneum Books, 2006.

Pirateology: The Sea Journal of Captain William Lubber. Dorking, United Kingdom: Templar Publishing, 2006.

Glossary

barnacle (BAHR-nuh-kuhl)—a crustacean (an animal like a lobster with a body covered by a hard shell) that lives in water and attaches itself to ship bottoms, rocks, pilings, and other objects

bow (BOW)—the front end of a boat or ship

broadside (BRAWD-side)—all of the cannons along one side of a ship firing together or in quick succession

buccaneer (buk-uh-NEER)—another name for pirate; derived from a French word meaning to smoke meat

careen (kuh–REEN)—to sail a ship onto the beach, pull it on its side, and then clean and repair the bottom

drydock (DRY-dawk)—a place where water could be temporarily removed so ship crews can work on the bottom of their ship

ferocious (fuh-ROH-shuhss)—savagely fierce or violently cruel

fleet (FLEET)—an organized unit of a number of ships

gulf (GULF)—part of the ocean partially surrounded by land

high tide (HIE TIDE)—when the level of the sea water is highest

indentured servant (in-DEHN-churd SIHR-vuhnt)—person who came to the Americas during the 1600s to 1800s with a contract to work for someone for five to seven years

low tide (LOE TIDE)—when the level of the sea water is lowest

mast (MAST)—on sailing ships, a large vertical pole to which the sails are attached

merchandise (MUR-chuhn-dice)–things that business people sell or buy

musket (MUHSS-kuht)—an early form of a rifle with a smooth bore

parley (PAHR-lee)—a form of conference and negotiation used to settle differences

pennant (PEHN-nuhnt)—a long, narrow, pointed flag

pilot (PIE-luht)—person who guides a ship in dangerous waters, based on knowledge of potential hazards

pistol (PIS-tuhl)—a short–barreled firearm

ramrod (RAM-rahd)—a thin metal rod used to push down the wadding, bullet, and explosive powder in a musket or pistol

retreat (ree-TREET)—withdrawal of a fighting force from battle to a safe place

sandbar (SAND-bahr)—a small island of sand created by currents and tides in a river or near the seashore

stern (stuhrn)—the back end of a boat or ship

teredo (tuh-REE-doe)—worm which attaches itself to the bottom of wooden ships and bores holes in the hull

tide (TIDE)—the rise and fall of ocean waters caused by the attraction of the moon and the sun

Index

About the Author

David Jay Derovan is an educator who grew up in Los Angeles, California. In 1983, he and his wife, Linda, and their two young boys moved to Israel and settled in Jerusalem. David continued to teach and to also work in graphics and public relations. The Derovans had three more children in Israel. Now, all of their children are married and have children of their own.

David has published numerous books and many articles. Since he was a small boy in California, David has been fascinated by pirates. He loves to draw pirate ships with all the details.